TODDLER COLORING BOOK

NUMBERS COLORS SHAPES

Baby Activity Book for Kids Age 1-3, Boys or Girls, for Their Fun Early Learning of First Easy Words about Shapes & Numbers, Counting While Coloring!

Olivia O. Arnett

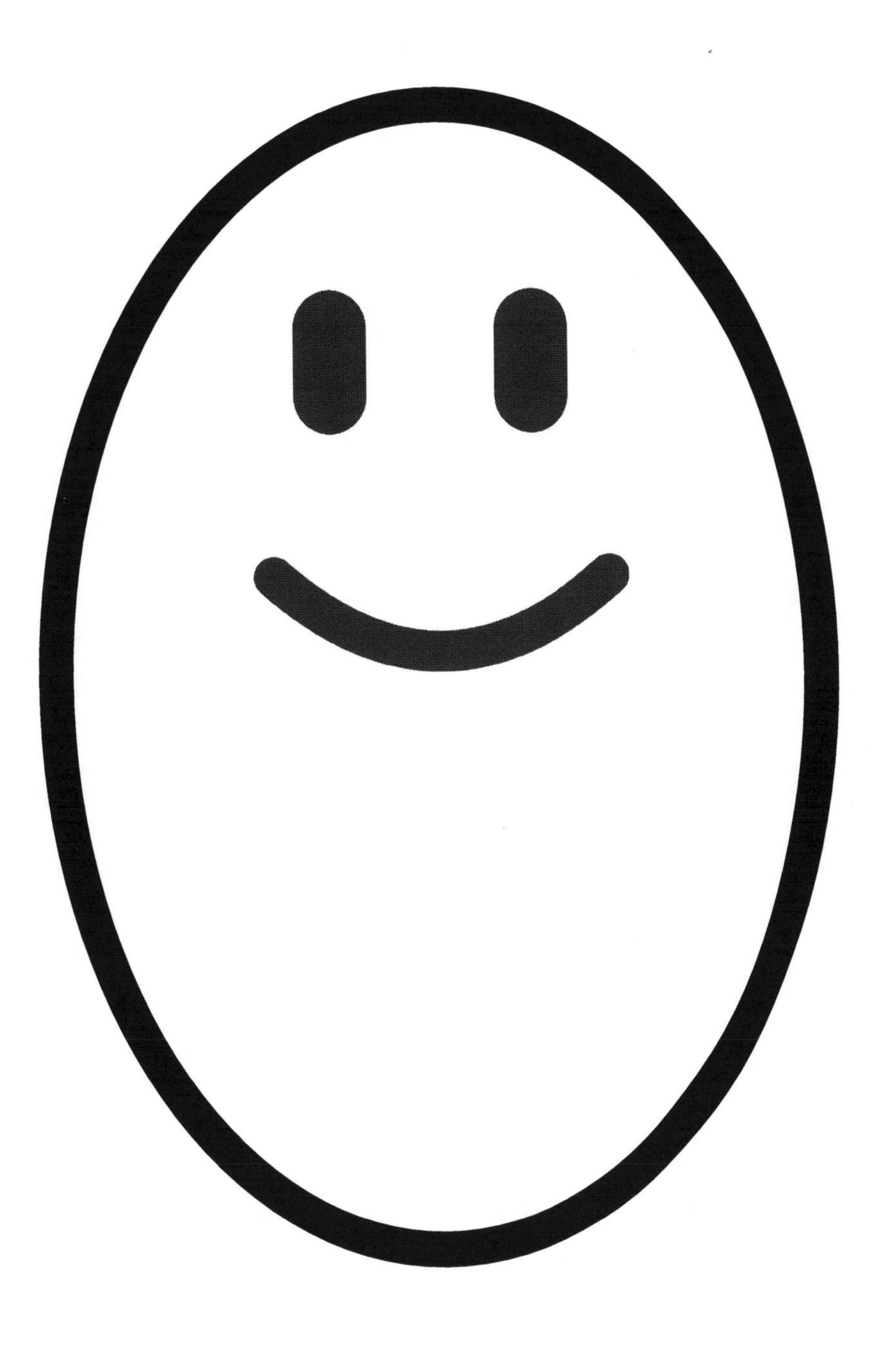

OVAL

SQUARE

RECTANGLE

TRIANGLE

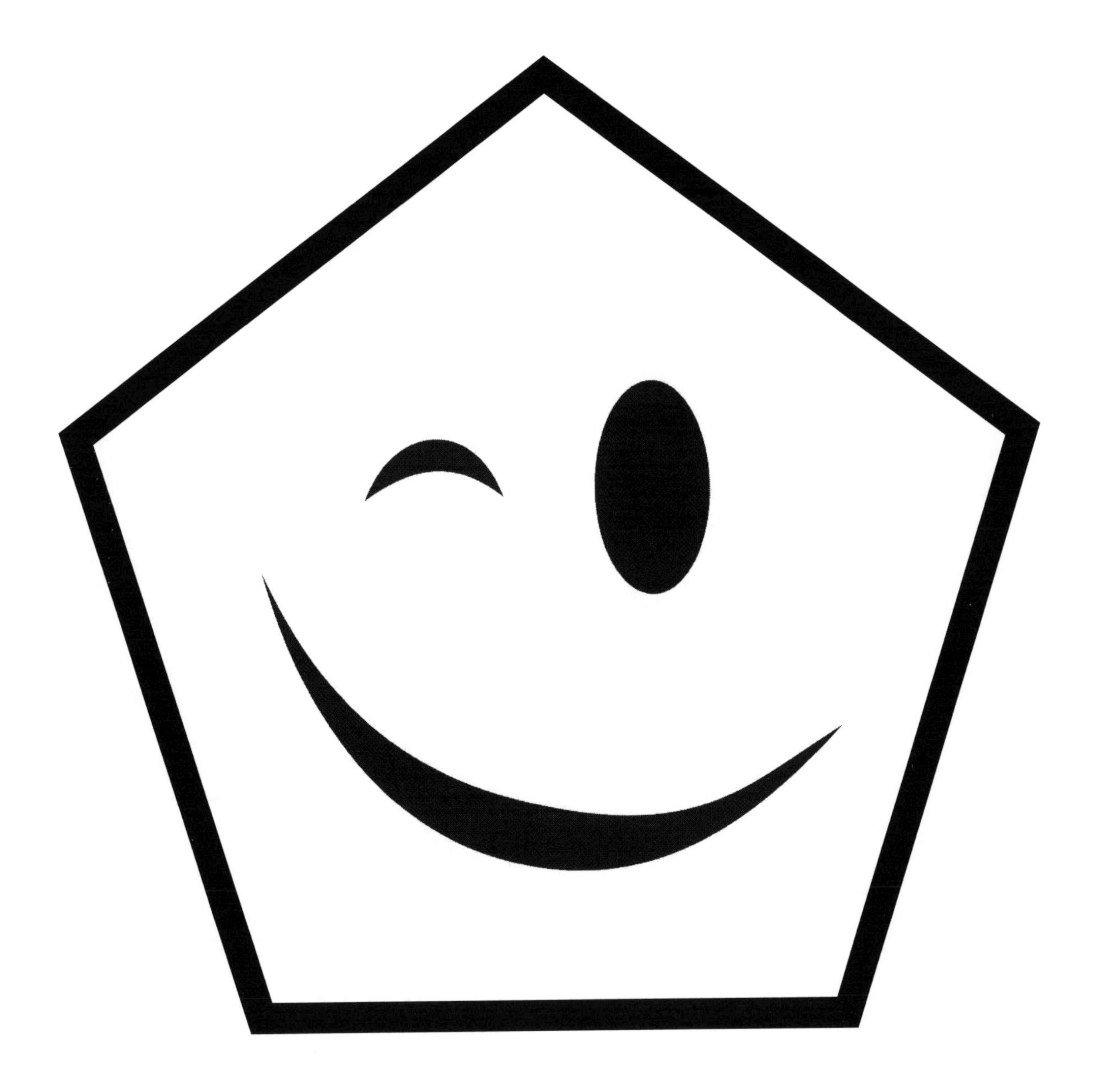

PENTAGON

STAR

HEART

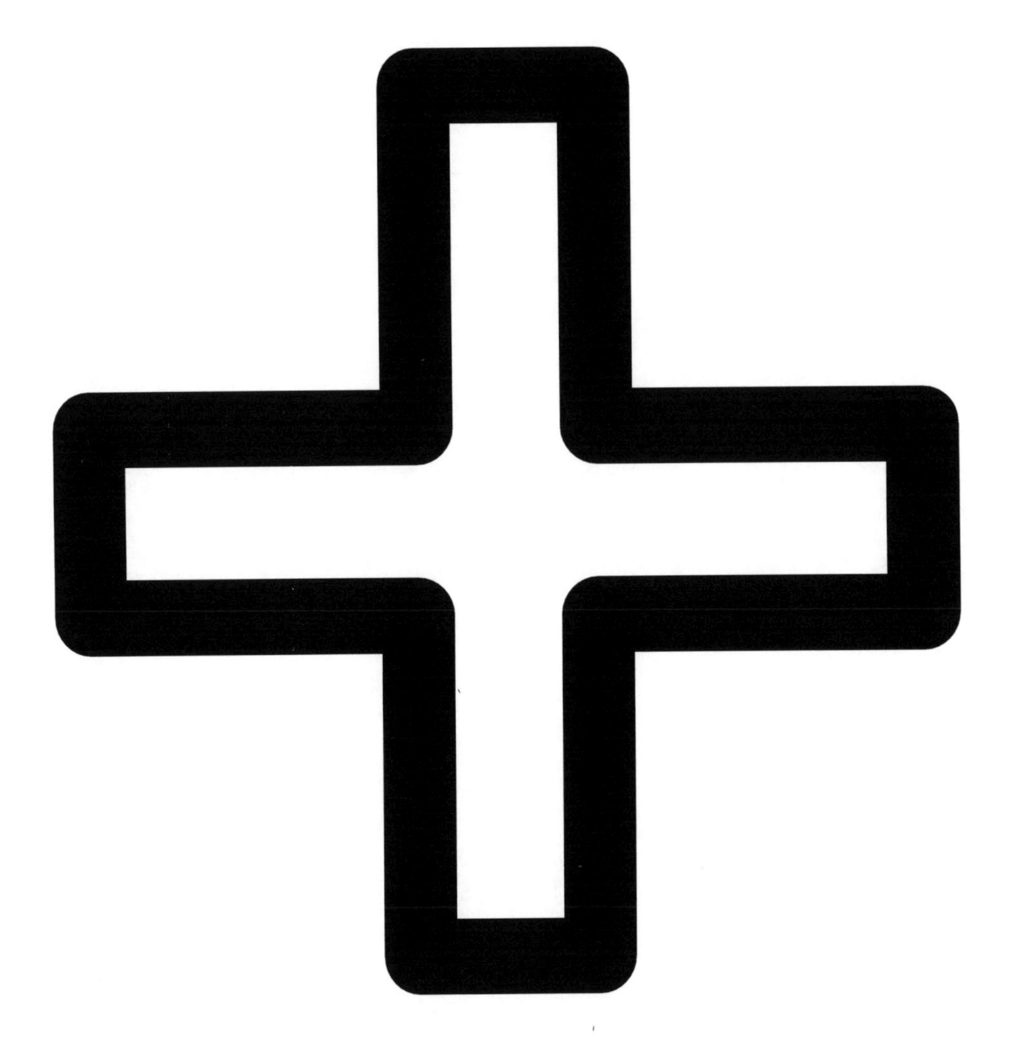

CROSS

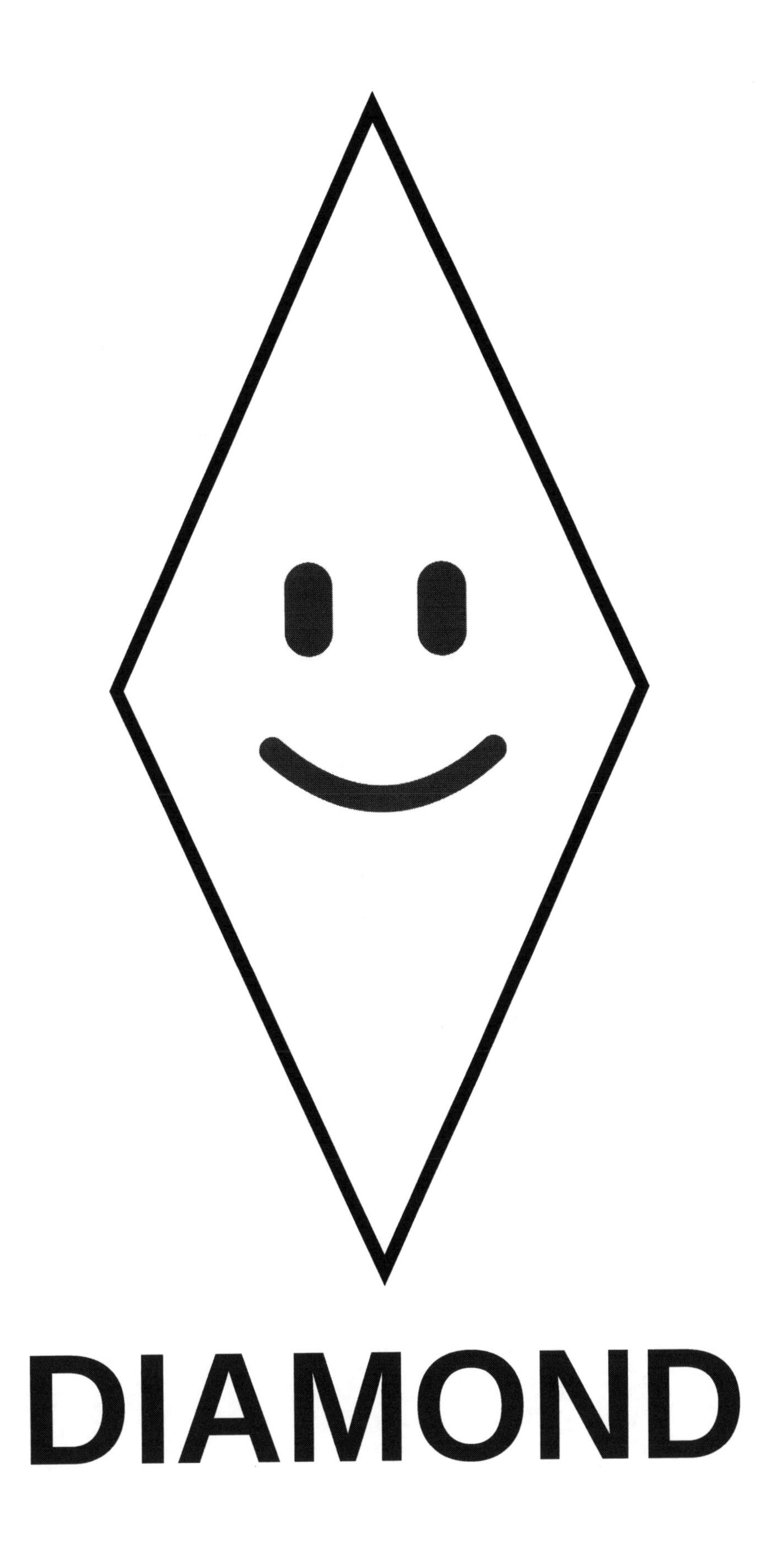
DIAMOND

ZERO

ONE

TWO

THREE

FOUR

FIVE

SIX

SEVEN

EIGHT

NINE

TEN

●●●●●●●●●●

ZERO = NOTHING

1 CIRCLE

2 OVALS

3 SQUARES

4 RECTANGLES

5 TRIANGLES

6 PENTAGONS

7 STARS

8 HEARTS

9 CROSSES

10 DIAMONDS

Thank you for your purchase of this book which is a part of the series "Preschool Prep Activity Learning", available at on-line and brick-and-mortar stores worldwide. We continuously strive for making books which are fun to read and exciting to learn, for our little angels of the world. We thank you so much again for your support!

Olivia O. Arnett

Made in the USA
Middletown, DE
18 December 2017